Think Big

Discover How To Expand Your Thinking In Order To Make Big Things Happen In Your Life

By Ace McCloud
Copyright © 2016

Disclaimer

The information provided in this book is designed to provide helpful information on the subjects discussed. This book is not meant to be used, nor should it be used, to diagnose or treat any medical condition. For diagnosis or treatment of any medical problem, consult your own physician. The publisher and author are not responsible for any specific health or allergy needs that may require medical supervision and are not liable for any damages or negative consequences from any treatment, action, application, or preparation, to any person reading or following the information in this book. Any references included are provided for informational purposes only. Readers should be aware that any websites or links listed in this book may change.

Table of Contents

Introduction 6

Chapter 1: Think Big and that is when the Magic Starts Happening 9

Chapter 2: Quell Fears & Celebrate Confidence 13

Chapter 3: Automate Life With Systems 17

Chapter 4: Attitude, Habits, and Work Ethic 20

Chapter 5: Goal-Setting and Leadership 29

Chapter 6: Thirty Days to Thinking Big 34

Chapter 7: Inspirational Story- Oprah: From Poverty to a Big Life 39

Chapter 8: Ace's Ultimate Bonus Tips 41

Conclusion 45

My Other Books and Audio Books 46

Be sure to check out my website for all my Books and Audio books.

www.AcesEbooks.com

Introduction

I want to thank you and congratulate you for buying the book, "Think Big: Discover How To Expand Your Thinking In Order To Make Big Things Happen In Your Life."

This book contains proven steps and strategies for making your helping make your greatest dreams come true by using the power of thinking big.

Thinking big is essential for success. Donald Trump and many others created empires by thinking big. They didn't decide to build slowly, one tiny bit at a time. They built empires by massive action and taking risks on immense dreams. Thinking big is what it takes to succeed in today's world and this book will help you do just that: think big, reach for the stars and then know what to do in order to reach your goals.

It is easy to become distracted by the small stuff and find yourself wrestling with trifling details when it would be better to focus on the overall objective. There are times when looking at the big picture can help you discover an all-encompassing solution that may just be the start to the life of your dreams. The tips and strategies in this book will help you build your life around a bigger picture so that you spend less time absorbed by the small stuff and more time focusing on the big picture.

Thinking big is a matter of perception:

- It involves believing you can accomplish your greatest objectives. Your overall vision isn't just a pipe dream, but reality in the making. We will take dead aim at the main distractions from thinking big and give practical suggestions to help you pursue your Big Idea.

- It includes viewing obstacles and difficulties as opportunities instead of problems or hassles. For example, let's say you have recently opened a restaurant and your meat vendor suddenly goes out of business. Rather than slamming your head up against a wall, look at this as a chance to find an even better supplier, one with higher quality products at better prices. You wouldn't have looked elsewhere if this situation had not arisen, so you might as well make the most of the opportunity. With the proper attitude, you can view any difficulty as a huge open door to refine your dream.

- It shifts your focus from what you cannot change to the million other possibilities. Let's say your Big Idea is to create an elegant restaurant in the best part of town, but the lease on the only available building is much higher than you can afford, in addition to being near three similar restaurants.

What are the other possibilities? Perhaps you discover an affordable property outside the city center near an upcoming mall? Can you find a way to make your dream work within this format?

One option is to offer upper-end menu choices at reasonable prices for the neighbors, but in an upscale atmosphere that is just opulent enough for middle class folks to feel special but not intimidated. You can still create the elegant dining experience you want. While not attracting opulent clientele, you might yet see more customers than would have been possible in the cut-throat competitive environment of the city. At the same time you could introduce a whole community to creative and unusual food choices they would not otherwise encounter.

Some may think "Why should I think big? Nothing good ever happens to me!" These are the types of thoughts that are useless and best disregarded as they hold no value.

There is a downside to not thinking big enough. I have a friend who wanted to own a goat farm where he could sell cheese and goat milk in the community. He already had a barn and a pasture and the land contained an outbuilding that could be refurbished to serve as a cheese and milk production house. However, he was afraid to go big, so he started out with only six goats.

My friend took out a loan to buy the goats and equip the barn with supplies and started construction on the outbuilding. The barn and pasture were large enough for fifty goats, but he had only six. Six goats were not enough to generate more than a day's worth of milk, let alone enough cheese to sell.

Because he didn't think big enough from the start, his dream fizzled and died. This caused my friend great pain because he had to sell the farm in order to pay back his loan. I truly believe that if he had taken out a larger loan so he could begin with even thirty goats, he would have been able to build a lucrative business. His cheese was really good; he just couldn't make a go of such a small enterprise.

This book is designed to help you start thinking in terms of the big picture and it will help you prepare yourself to pursue your large-as-life objectives. You will encounter several individuals just like you who have been able to make good on their Big Ideas. They may have been frustrated at times as they pursued their dream, but they were able to attain success because they were not satisfied with a mere six goats. They started out with a full head of steam and risked everything in order to achieve their Big Idea.

In one chapter of this book we will highlight Oprah Winfrey, a mega-success story and an ongoing big thinker in her own right. From an unassuming beginning, she made it big through determination and by continually setting her sights on a Big Idea.

Follow your dreams. You will always be a lot more eager to get up in the morning when you're chasing your heart. This book will help you define what's in your heart to pursue, what you were wired for, and then strategies for making that dream come true. These chapters will help you to tune your perceptions to your heart's desire and follow that Big Idea. Included are practical exercises and world class action strategies that will help you along the way.

Thinking big leads to greater satisfaction in life. Pursuing a Big Idea will steer you away from the path of the mediocre person who just floats down the river of life, never daring to truly live. Think Big and Feel the Satisfaction of knowing you are pursuing your Greatest Desires and that You are something Greater than yourself, that you are the Leader of a Winning Team of Your Own Choosing!

Chapter 1: Think Big and that is when the Magic Starts Happening

David Schwartz wrote "The Magic of Thinking Big" back in 1959, but the thoughts, techniques, and even outcomes are as valid today as they were years ago. In his book, Schwartz studies the steps of thinking big that lead to the end result of success. He emphasizes setting high goals and thinking in a positive manner to reach those goals. This book shows just how timeless some of the great success secrets are. This book was a lot of fun to listen to on audio book.

As we continue through this book, we will further explain the magic of thinking big in the context of your goals, your confidence, fears, and life structure, as well as your perceptions and attitudes. I will provide help in setting larger than life goals and will also offer an easy to do 30-day strategy complete with some great examples. Along the way, we will learn from others who have been able to think big and dare big things.

The video, The Magic of Thinking big by David Schwartz, posted on YouTube by Brian Johnson, will give you some of the objectives of David Schwartz and explain why thinking big is magic.

First, let's look at the attributes of someone who thinks big so you can identify and emulate them.

- Big-thinkers are **innovative**. They look "outside the box" for solutions to problems. They think of unique ways to get what they need and are often noticed as leaders in society.

- Big thinkers are **imaginative**. They come up with solutions that no one else can see. They have the ability to imagine themselves in a situation and, from the inside, find the best way out of it.

- Big thinkers are **creative**. They can make a luscious dinner out of a box of macaroni and cheese, using what they already have in the kitchen. Their creative minds can imagine the light at the end of the tunnel before it can be seen. These individuals are eager to press forward with the implementation of their ideas

- Big thinkers have **thick skin**. Everyone encounters naysayers occasionally, but those who think big come up against opposition all the time. Big thinkers develop a thick skin and let the negative comments roll right off their backs.

  Thick skin is a learned trait; we don't come by it naturally. It is only human to care about what others think of us. A big thinker, however, has enough confidence in what she has been called to do that she is free to look into the words of the naysayers for ways to improve, all without being swayed from her purpose.

Let's look at some of the big thinkers in the world:

- **You're never too old** – There really was a Colonel Sanders. He had an idea that we know today as Kentucky Fried Chicken. The Colonel really was an old man with white hair who wore a white suit.

    When he was 65, Colonel Sanders discovered he was not content with the $105 check he received each month from Social Security. He hatched an idea: Why not sell his chicken recipe to a large corporation? He traveled all over the country, slept in his car, and knocked on 1,009 doors before a restaurateur let him in to make his famous chicken in the kitchen. The results of the man who dreamed big and pursued that dream incessantly? He created a multi-million dollar empire, built on fried chicken!

- **Daydreaming pays off** – Do you remember the kid who didn't pay much attention in school and always got yelled at by the teacher for daydreaming? Was that kid you? If so, you already have inside you a skill that others would pay millions to own.

    Walt Disney was one such dreamer. He was never good in school and was fired from his job as a newspaper editor for his "lack of imagination." Yes, this was the man who came up with the big eared black and white mouse that sang and danced; he did not have any imagination they said!

    Disney's first animation company failed, but he persevered until his mouse dream became something really big.

- **Perseverance is key** – Big thinkers do not give up. Thomas Edison wasn't supposed to amount to anything according to his teachers and his family. He was fired from his first two jobs because they said he was unproductive. However, the man had stick-to-it-iveness! He had a dream that he just *knew* would work and he wouldn't quit until he had figured it out. After 1,000 attempts, Thomas Edison finally created a light bulb that worked. Now, *that* is perseverance!

- **"Never give in"** (Winston Churchill) – This story celebrates the persistence of friends. Stephen King's first book "Carrie" was rejected thirty times. He was so frustrated that he threw the manuscript in the trash. However, King's wife pulled the papers out, brushed off a few stray potato peels, and convinced her husband to try just one more time. Thank God she did! I cannot conceive of a world without Stephen King novels.

- **Do what it takes** – (within the bounds of ethics and legality, of course). Lucille Ball was persistent. She also had the ability to take lemons and make lemonade.

  Lucille, or "Lucy" as she came to be known, was a failed actress who had only worked in low budget B-rated movies, but she had a dream to be a star. She was a beautiful woman, but indistinguishable from all the other gorgeous blondes out there. In a stroke of – craziness? genius? – she dyed her hair bright red and adopted a zany personality. That got her noticed, alright!

  During her career as a TV star and comedienne, Lucy was nominated for thirteen Emmy awards, four of which she won. Lucille Ball, former nobody, was also honored at the Kennedy Center with a Lifetime Achievement Award.

- **Grow with your dream** – Oprah is another entertainer who made it big because of being a big thinker. She was not satisfied to remain a newscaster. Even after achieving her dream of becoming a household name, she set her sights on new dreams. She went on to build the HARPO empire, then founded the Angel Network, and has since helped millions of people around the world.

So, how do you start to think big? Ask yourself:

1. **How can I do this better?** Colonel Sanders probably asked himself if his fried chicken was the best it could possibly be before he stepped out to try and sell the recipe.

2. **Is there a more creative angle to approach my idea?** Lucy acted in several B-rated movies, but that did not satisfy her. She got creative in order to birth a new persona that caused people to sit up and take notice. Lucy has since worked her way into the hearts of millions.

3. **How can I take this idea of mine to a higher level?** Walt Disney started with an animation company and could have stayed there. Instead, he built a fantasy empire with a presence that spans the globe. He discovered that it is indeed, "a small world after all."

4. **How I can expand my dream?** Don't be satisfied with a single bed and breakfast. Go for a chain of them all over the world.

Don't delay. Once you develop your Big Idea as far as possible, it is important to start working on it, yes, today. Don't let the grass grow under your feet. Hesitation may lead to contentment with the status quo. The comfort of grass between your toes is soothing. Before long, the love of comfort will have swallowed up your dream.

Say "No!" to excuses. Your mind will invent all sorts of reasons to avoid moving forward with your big idea. No, you *don't* have to wait until the children get older. You *don't* have to wait until you have made enough money to start setting things in motion. Ignore these paralyzing ideas and power on forward.

Use visualization to cement that Big Idea in place inside you. Set aside fifteen minutes before bed. Find a place where you will not be disturbed. Sit straight upright in a chair; avoid lying down or you just might fall asleep and miss the benefits of this exercise. Close your eyes and visually imagine yourself waking up tomorrow. You get up, get dressed, do your morning ritual, and then head to work. When you arrive at your workplace, visualize yourself in the role you are aiming for in your dreams. Start with where you are now in your life and envision the path you can travel from where you are to where you want to be.

Dwell on the point where you have realized your dream in all its glory. How will you solve the problems inherent with this new role? The visualization of successful problem-solving can increase your confidence in your dream and in your worthiness to achieve it.

Your actual life path may not turn out exactly like your visualizations, but what you envision will pave the way for *any* path that reaches toward your dreams.

Be willing to flex your plans. Don't be afraid to change in order to meet the situations that crop up in your life. Perhaps you may imagine yourself as the president of a prestigious university, even though you haven't been able to graduate because of family and money issues. However, you can keep your dream alive by creatively and persistently working toward that first step of graduation. You can pursue a GED online, and many universities will allow you to take a class at a time, working bit by bit toward graduation. As long as you never give up, your goal is still alive.

Chapter 2: Quell Fears & Celebrate Confidence

Thinking big isn't as easy to do as you may think. You must first let go of all those safety mechanisms your mind has set up over the years. You'll need to learn when to ignore those alarm bells that warn you away; after all, they're only trying to protect you. People who think big are not ruled by their fear, however. They power through any anxiety or misgivings and go for the gold. Big thinkers also have self-confidence. They know they can do it!

Fear and lack of confidence are two of the largest obstacles to thinking big. Until you conquer your fear and develop some confidence, your progress toward your dream will be frequently waylaid.

The Myth of Security

It is normal for humans to desire safety. That is why so many of us remain in a job we don't enjoy or hang on, even when we know we can't advance in the current job. We seek security and avoid change. Because change feels uncomfortable, it is easy to believe that anything different might do us harm.
We prefer to think small in order to preserve a false sense of control.

I cannot tell you how many people I know who have remained in dead end jobs for years, simply because it was secure and comfortable. They went to work every day, did the same thing every day, and came home at the same time every night. They never looked any further because they were secure; or were they?

Control of our lives is a myth. How many of those people ended up losing their jobs when their company changed hands, folded or downsized? Quite a few of them were forced into a world of change, against their wishes. What they had sacrificed in terms of full-blooded living in order to have security, turned out to be grasping for the wind.

Sometimes we are afraid of being an outcast or being ridiculed. I'm sure Thomas Edison was looked upon as quite daft when he told everyone he could make light shine in a tiny glass bulb. Fortunately for us, he didn't care what anyone said or how many times he failed. He just kept on going, with or without fear. He had enough confidence to persevere until he succeeded.

<u>Overcoming Fear</u>

There is a small, almond shaped pod in the middle of the human brain called the amygdala. It is the part of our brain that processes our first reaction to fear. When fear strikes, the amygdala speeds up the heart and makes muscles tense up in anticipation of fight or flight. This is the most primitive part of the brain and it is also present in animals. The amygdala, also called the reptilian brain, only has the rudimentary ability to run or fight when confronted with what it deems a threat.

Fortunately, humans have other areas in our brain that allow us to evaluate the fight-or-flight instinct and choose appropriate responses. The trick to overcoming fear is to step out of the reptilian brain and into the cognitive sections of our mind to take control of our responses.

There are several ways you can develop your control of any fears that crop up when you are thinking big.

Breathing exercises are very useful in controlling the flight or fight reflex of the reptilian brain. To start with, find a quiet place. Sit or stand still in a relaxed but alert posture. Concentrate on breathing. When you feel fear start to invade your thoughts, pause, then breath in slowly for a count of five. Hold your breath for another five counts and exhale slowly for five counts. Repeat this process until you are calm. This exercise distracts the reptilian brain and disconnects it for a moment, just long enough for you to take control.

Visualization can also help put a stop to your fears. Some people have a place they love to go to relax and feel good. Keep a mental image of your favorite place and when fear starts to creep into your thoughts stop, breathe deeply, and go to that place in your mind. Visualize yourself there and immerse yourself in refreshment by using all of your senses . If your favorite place is the beach, feel the warmth of the sun on your skin and the breeze wafting your hair, smell the salt air, look at the beauty and power of the ocean, and feel the texture of the sand between your toes. This exercise also distracts the reptilian brain and allows you to gain control again.

Dietary supplements can actually lessen the anxiety that comes with fear. If you feel you need a little more help beyond breathing and visualization, you can try the following supplements and see if your fears become more manageable:

- St. John's Wort is probably the most well-known herb used to combat anxiety and depression; it can help you conquer small fears. The active ingredient in the herb is hypericin, which can lift spirits. St. John's Wort works a bit quicker than other remedies; you will feel positive effects within a few weeks rather than a few months. The supplement is easily accessible in capsule form at most pharmacies and health food stores. Keep in mind that St. John's Wort tends to reduce the effectiveness of birth control and increases sun sensitivity.

- Vitamin B is thought to alleviate and reduce instances of panic attacks by affecting nerve functionality and boosting one's mood. Vitamin B deficiency is common in many people, but supplement pills can help raise the levels. Vitamin B1 moderates the blood sugar while B3 creates serotonin, which aids in sleep. Even controlling your blood sugar goes a long ways toward controlling your mood and helps to combat anxiety while Serotonin brings tranquility. Vitamin B5 helps adrenal function and

B12 is thought to combat depression. Try a B-complex supplement for best results.

Confidence

Lack of confidence is one of the biggest big dream killers around. It is literally impossible to think big without having confidence in yourself. "Why should I consider doing this when I know it just isn't in me?" you might ask. That kind of shrinking back often has as much to do with lack of confidence as it does with fear.

Confidence helps you reject the ideas of a group and enables you to strive to be who you really are, a complete unique individual. Complete people are more likely to be big thinkers. Confidence will allow you to realize you have a purpose in life and it can nudge you to accomplish goals toward that purpose.

Know yourself. Celebrate the uniqueness that makes you, you. None of us are meant to live identical lives. We have unique fingerprints, unique brainwaves, unique dreams. Therefore, don't fear being different from others. Instead focus on the positive aspects of who you are. You are uniquely suited to realize your Big Idea.

Take care of your body. Physical exercise, strength training, and healthy eating make up the foundation for self-confidence. You don't have to be a world-class athlete; just manage your body by training it to serve you.

Optimizing your physical well-being is essential to any other pursuit. It can give you the physical, mental, and emotional stamina you need to pursue your goals. The better shape your body is in, the more you will *want* to pursue your dreams. Healthy living can provide a huge boost to your self-confidence.

Remember your successes. It's tempting to wallow in negative past experiences. However, by choosing to think about times when you performed at your best, you can actually boost your desire to push forward into the future. For example, think about a time you did something great at work or school. Remember what you did to get there and how good it felt when you had arrived? While remembering a past success, it is easier to feel confident in your current pursuit.

Journal positive experiences. Write down your events where you succeeded. Include pictures, awards, news clippings, or anything else that reminds you of past achievements or things that just make you happy. Then, read through this journal to keep your spirits high. I suggest daily marking your stopping place with a bookmark so you pick up your reading next time where you left off.

Here are some additional things you can do to increase your confidence and banish your fears:

- **Stay positive**; practicing turning any negative thought into a positive one.

- **Help others** by serving them. Volunteer at a soup kitchen. You will soon see your importance to others and this will boost your confidence.

- **Know and accept your weaknesses**. Respect your limits but don't be bound by them.

  We all have weaknesses, but that doesn't mean we will have them forever. When I was young, I had little confidence and was very shy. One day I decided that wouldn't do, so I concentrated on being more outgoing. I swallowed my fear by signing up to be on the debate team at school. Now I can speak in front of thousands without too much fear. Accept your weaknesses and find ways to turn them into strengths.

- **Find love.** Your self-confidence will blossom when you are loved. Any love will do; romantic love, the love of a child, respect from coworkers and affection from friends and family will banish fear and boost your confidence.

Check out this video on confidence called How to be More Confident – A step-by-step Process for Becoming Truly Confident by Actualized.org. Learn about overcoming fear with the video Reprogramming your brain to overcome fear: Olympia LePoint at TEDxPCC by TEDxTalks.

Removing fear and welcoming confidence is the first step in becoming a big thinker. Find success in this and you are well on your way to achieving your Big Idea.

Chapter 3: Automate Life With Systems

To pursue your big idea, you will need to free up as much of your time, mental energy and physical stamina as possible. You can accomplish this by automating almost every highly repetitive area of life. Automation, including the automation of frequent habits, will free your attention from quite a few mundane tasks. When you automate what you can, life runs much more smoothly and your steps toward thinking big and attaining your goals can progress seamlessly.

Computer Maintenance

Few of us actually do these things until we've faced the potential – or actual – loss of important information. Keeping your computer optimized will add years to its life expectancy. When you keep your files backed up regularly, you also run less risk of losing valuable items.

Set up a schedule for computer maintenance. Some maintenance activities can be scheduled to occur automatically. Set them up to run late at night, when no one is using the computer.

- Clear out your old emails periodically. You may want to also clear out deleted emails, spam, and draft messages.

- Run defragmentation and backup programs on a regular basis, if they are not automatically run by your virus checker.

- Your virus protection software should be set to run virus checks once a week, in addition to automatically checking anything incoming.

- Clean your computer of any malware or spyware by downloading an application such as CCleaner; schedule it to run every week.

- Back up your files to an external hard drive or to cloud space once a week.

Automate Bill Payments

Most financial institutions allow you to schedule automated payments on monthly bills. You can schedule your mortgage payment for the same day each month. You can request your bank's program to remind you when it is time to pay bills that vary in amount from month to month. Any recurring bill can be set up for automatic payment. This works especially well for people who are paid on a regular basis. If your income is fairly steady, this is an excellent way to free yourself from the hassles of manually paying your bills.

Direct Deposit

Get paid via direct deposit whenever possible. This eliminates trips to the bank and waiting in long lines on payday. It also puts the money in your hands immediately. Most employers prefer to process paychecks via direct deposit. All an employer needs to set this up is your account number and the routing number of your bank.

Paperless Bills

Instead of waiting for the postal service to deliver bills to your house, opt to receive them via email. Some banks will link with utility companies to display your bills on your personal banking site and will notify you when a new bill has arrived. Going paperless not only saves trees, but it will save much time and aggravation. You never have to worry about misplacing a bill or having it get lost in the mail. If you want a hard copy, you can always print it yourself or request one from the institution.

Another benefit of paperless bills is security. There is less chance of someone grabbing a bill from your garbage can or mail box and stealing your identity. Ensure that your computer has a good security system so your paperless bills will also be safe.

More Ways to Go Paperless

- Use a scanner to store paper bills and other documents onto your computer. Scan, then shred or lock away the paper version.

- Scan receipts and store them in your computer. Set up a good keyword search system so you can find what you need quickly.

- Store your recipes on your computer by either scanning or typing them in.

- Keep notes on your computer.

- Maintain your calendar on your computer and/or on your smart phone.

- Download magazine subscriptions in any kind of e-reader.

You will be much better organized by digitizing everything you can. Just make sure to back everything up regularly. No computer lasts forever and you never know when your hard drive might act up.

Automate Your Shopping

- Start by digitizing your favorite recipes. The more recipes you can store on the computer, the easier it will be to plan both your weekly meals and shopping trips. You can save your recipes in folders on your computer or

Google Docs, or you can check out any of the many software options available.

- Find a meal planning program for the computer or an app for your smart phone. You will be surprised at how much time you can save by automating your meal planning. Create a digital shopping list for your meals so you can go to the store once instead of three or four times because you forgot essential items.

- Plan your meals with current online ads in mind. For example, if chicken is on sale, punch in chicken when you search your recipes. You can save tons of time here, which can be better spent on big thinking and planning.

- Subscription shopping is another way to save time. When you need hairspray or toothpaste, do you walk in a store and just go get that hairspray or toothpaste? That isn't very likely. A store visit usually means you will spend precious time looking at things you don't need and you can easily spend money unnecessarily. If you set up a subscription service for those items, they will be automatically sent to you. You may even get a big discount on them. Subscription services can include toiletries, pharmaceuticals, and sometimes even groceries.

- Some grocery stores will let you fax or email a shopping list and they will deliver it locally or have it ready for pickup.

Here are some additional tasks that can be at least partially automated:

- If you have a dishwasher, use it. It's all the better if you can persuade everyone in the house to rinse their dishes as soon as they are finished eating and load them in the dishwasher. When it's full, load the soap and turn it on.

- Use an automated vacuum to clean your floors while you do other things.

- Use your cell phone to set your thermostat or the security system in your home.

- Use digital calendars to schedule appointments and events; and set alarm reminders to go off well before the event or appointment.

Use [Microsoft OneNote](#) or other similar program. I won't go into all the details in this book, but I have been able to set up my whole life like a mastermind genius on OneNote. I can't recommend it enough. If you want to know more be sure to check out my book on it, it is really great!

Automate your life to give yourself more time for big thinking and planning. Save your energies for things that are most important using the 80/20 rule of success.

Chapter 4: Attitude, Habits, and Work Ethic

Attitude, habits, and work ethics go hand in hand for a big thinker. Each of these things is essential to the success of your Big Idea.

Attitude

Life is all about attitude. If you have a positive attitude, stuff seems to fall into place and things eventually work out for you. A positive attitude gives you the ability to turn things around if they are unsatisfactory. So what if you can't afford that building for your restaurant in an upscale part of town? A positive, confident attitude opens the door so you can retool your plan to start an upscale restaurant franchise in the suburbs. Often your Big Idea will work out well, but in a way you never dreamed it would happen.

If life has dealt you a hard blow you may find it difficult to look at anything in positive terms. When all illusions of control have been shattered, it is only natural to approach all aspects of life with skepticism. This is a survival mechanism built into our bodies to help keep us alive in times of crisis. However, once the immediate crisis has abated, this perspective can persist, coloring the way we view the world around us. This extreme, binary-based way of thinking can easily become our reality. If it *looks* like reality, we usually think it *is* reality.

If you find yourself forgetting that a half-empty glass can be refilled, it is time for an attitude adjustment. Here are some things you can do to start reframing reality in a more positive light:

Look for it. Choose to discover at least one positive trait of each person you encounter in your day. Instead of criticizing or demonizing, remind yourself that every person you meet is a human being just like yourself.

Find alternatives. When you encounter a setback, take time to catch your breath, take stock of what you still have that you can work with, and find a next step forward toward your goal. A friend of mine has been going to college on and off for six years, working on a library science degree. During her final year of school she developed a problem with her eyes and became partially blind, to the extent that she could not read. Most people would have given up and quit school, but she went on to learn braille and is now pursuing a career as a teacher and librarian for the blind. She didn't quit. She took stock of her situation and found a way to move forward toward her dream.

Live in the Now. Stop dwelling on the past or dreaming about the future. The only thing you can change is the present, the here and now, so don't miss out on a minute of it. Your choices and actions in the present are your most precious possession, because by acting in the present, you are laying a foundation for your future.

While this may seem like a simple paragraph in a book, it is one of the most important things you can ever master. George MacDonald calls it "the sacred present." Learn how to live in the "now" for increased happiness and a positive attitude. Watch Eric Tran's [Eckhart Tolle Interview By Oprah on The Power of Now YouTube](), to truly realize the power of living in the moment. Once again, this may be a very small part of the book... but if you truly take the time to put this principle into your life you will be much happier in the long run and succeed at a higher rate and level.

Avoid negative words like "can't" or "won't." Using the positive terms, "can" and "will" helps your mind shift towards a more practical framework. Consistent use of positive terms will over time move your mind to start thinking in terms of your capabilities. Then all sorts of possibilities will open up to you.

Don't give up. There is something to one of my very favorite children's story and early Saturday cartoon, "The Little Engine that Could". The train was able to make his way to the top of a long steep hill just by repeating the iconic words, "I think I can, I think I can" over and over again. That little engine just refused to give up!

I can't tell you how many successful people have become superstars, just because they refused to give up. They never gave up on a play. They never gave up on a day. They never gave up on their beliefs. They never gave up on themselves. They just kept on pushing forward.

Some people call it heart; others call it willpower or tenacity. What it all boils down to is developing an unwavering belief in yourself and your goals, and then moving toward them each day while never giving in. Some days will be better than others, but that choice to keep moving forward is a common trait of all the great men and women throughout history.

Choose how you respond to impending change. There are four basic ways to view change:

- Enthusiastically embrace it. Some people naturally thrive on change. If you are one of these people, be glad. The only danger with this attitude is to embrace change for change's sake, without adequately examining both the advantages and disadvantages of said change.

- Grudging acceptance. This is a dangerous position, both for yourself and for the people around you. If you don't like a specific change, but view it as inevitable, it is easy to view yourself as a victim of the inevitable However, you *do* have a choice in the matter: You can choose to accept that this change is inevitable and start working to find ways to live with it; you can influence the change, shaping it into something you can live with; you can choose to remove yourself from the situation entirely, or you can choose to resist.

Whatever you do, please don't stay in this attitude indefinitely. Grudging acceptance is a wet blanket on everybody around you. If you don't choose eventually to shift your attitude toward acceptance, you will find yourself stuck, mired in a very unpleasant present.

- Resistance is another possible attitude toward change. Sometimes we have an instinctive knee-jerk reaction against a proposed change. Usually such an instinctive response is caused by something deep within that we may or may not fully understand. It is a signal that warrants a step back and some careful consideration. There may be grave danger ahead, and your "spidey senses" are simply warning you. Whatever the case, before you commit yourself to openly opposing the looming change, it's a good idea to check out why you feel like resisting it.

- The fourth option, and the one I recommend, is to accept your initial response as valid. But don't stop there. Evaluate the situation, looking for what is behind your enthusiastic embrace, grudging acceptance, or vehement opposition. After you fully comprehend everything the change will entail, then you can deliberately plan your response. Just remember, that action, even if you fail, is almost always better than taking no action at all, as at least you can learn from your mistakes and move forward. When in doubt, do your research and model an expert in whatever you are trying to do.

Choose a positive attitude. Yes, your attitude is a choice. Your current attitude may have been chosen so long ago that you forgot about it. But you do have the authority – at any moment – to choose the angle from which you view things.

The power of attitude is not always understood. Negative attitudes foster anxiety, anger, bitterness, and envy. When those emotions take hold they can influence your decisions for the worse. When, on the other hand, you adopt a positive attitude, your reactions to life events tend to be positive. For example, if your child is misbehaving, your love for her will lead you to handle the situation with more compassion and kindness than if you are only thinking about how much it irritates you. The same holds true for a variety of other situations.

Feed your attitude with affirmations. Affirmations are words and sentences you speak to yourself in order to reframe your underlying attitudes. Some examples of positive affirmations are:

- I deserve to be happy.

- I am smart and organized enough to get a good-paying job.

- I am worthy of love.

- I see the good in all people and situations.
- I love my life.
- I am generous, giving, and caring.
- I act quickly and decisively.
- I am going to be a winner today.
- I will grow today by following good habits, eating healthy food and pursuing positive relationships.
- I am strong, healthy, wealthy and wise.
- I am super creative and perform flawlessly.

I encourage you to create your your own affirmations that pertain to your goals and needs and that will reinforce the positive attitudes you want to build into your life.

Affirmations build confidence. If you tell yourself you can do a task, you are more likely to complete it. I knew a teacher who worked at an inner city high school where the kids were considered very unlikely to succeed. Teachers left by the droves because they just couldn't handle the discipline problems there.

My friend was a tiny woman, at first glance someone very unlikely to succeed at this school. Every day she would enter the school with her head held high and each morning she would start the day with a set of positive affirmations she and her homeroom students had devised. Some of her classroom affirmations were:

- I will be kind to my fellow students and my teachers.
- I will learn something new today.
- I deserve a good education.
- I can succeed if I try.

The kids thought it was pretty stupid at first and many mocked her and her affirmations, but she kept it up and did not waver. Pretty soon the kids were repeating her affirmations and calling out their own for the class to repeat. She rarely had trouble with the students and they were her most loyal protectors.

This woman taught there for 25 years before retiring. She ultimately changed the lives of thousands of students, all because of positive affirmations.

Habits

We all know about habits. The experts say it takes about 21 days of consistent repetition to build a habit, whether you are stopping a bad habit or building a new one. For any habit adjustment you require a motivation that is more powerful than the cost of remaining the same. The only way to truly change is to see that the cost down the road of remaining the same is greater than the discomfort and hassle you will endure in order to change.

If you are determined to make a change, here are some practical aids that help:

Be Consistent. Consistency is key when trying to learn a new habit. If you do not practice your habit every day, or at least a few times a week, you risk the chance of it not setting into a permanent part of your life. For example, if you want to make a habit of brushing your teeth every morning when you first wake up, it will not do to brush your teeth only on the days you feel like it. It will require willpower and determination to get up every morning and make yourself head straight to the sink. However, by paying the price for three weeks, ensuring that you brush your teeth first thing every morning, you will soon begin to perform this on "autopilot", without having to fight contrary desires every day you wake up.

Write About It. When you write something down, you are more likely to remember it or at least keep it in the back of your mind. By writing down your goal to internalize a habit, it may be easier to remember to actively pursue the change. Then, whenever you are feeling tempted to give up, you can refer back to what you wrote and remind yourself why you decided to make this change in the first place. It may prove helpful to keep a habit-forming journal. Use it to write about your progress and your thoughts on forming new habits. This can be very inspirational. If you don't want to make a journal, at the very least write your objective on a piece of paper, along with your "why" for pursuing this change, and post it in a place where you can review it daily.

Visualize. Visualization is a powerful boost to building new habits. If you have ever read about goal-setting, you have probably heard the advice to visualize yourself achieving your goal. Building a habit is no different, because it *is* a goal.

By thinking about what your life will be like once you've established a new habit, you may feel more inspired and energized to persevere. Since visualization is such a valuable strategy, I recommend you check out this YouTube video, "how to visualize your goals" by Howdini.

Another visualization exercise is to view the scenario in the third person. Pretend you are observing yourself performing your new habit, watching from a distance. Studies have shown that this tactic can increase the power of your visualization.

To avoid tricking your brain into prematurely thinking your habit is set, you should also visualize yourself performing each detail of the habit you plan to establish. For example, visualize yourself from a distance setting your alarm, ensuring that you have adequate toothpaste available and a fresh toothbrush. Watch yourself from a distance as you wake, stand up and walk to the bathroom sink, open the toothpaste, pick up the toothbrush, etc.

Pick a Role Model. It is not always easy to make a change in your life on your own. One good way to stay focused is to pick a role model. Your role model may not be famous for brushing her teeth every day, but they should be someone who has overcome obstacles in order to achieve success. Choose a hero and let their persistence carry over into your truly big goals. My two favorite role models have always been Arnold Schwarzenegger and Tony Robins.

Eliminate Temptation. To better absorb a new habit, get rid of anything that can interrupt or interfere with your progress. As you probably know, temptation is, well, tempting. You may give in thinking, "it's only this one time," but it's easy to lose track of how many "one times" you've given in. Enough times and you'll be building another habit: the habit of giving in to temptation. When you decide to build a new habit, one of your first actions should be to eliminate or plan how to deal with temptation. For example, if you're trying to form a habit of eating better, clear all the junk food out of your house and decide what you're going to do when a friend or the nearest vending machine entices you with those Twinkies.

Substitute an Activity. If you are trying to break a bad habit, it can be easier to abandon if you fill the gap with a new, positive habit. For example, if you're trying to quit smoking but you're used to smoking while you watch TV, find something else to do during your TV time. You could chew gum, sip water, massage your feet, or otherwise find a way to occupy your hands and distract yourself. An alternate activity will occupy your mind, so you won't be bombarded as badly with thoughts of smoking.

Develop a Trigger. If you've ever taken a basic psychology class, you've probably heard of triggers before. A trigger sends a signal to your brain, telling it to do something. You can create a trigger to help you stick to learning a new habit. For example, if you want to stop biting your nails, clap your hands together whenever you feel the urge to bite your nails. When you clap your hands and refrain from biting your nails, your brain will eventually learn to associate clapping with no nail biting. Another good trigger is to paste some pictures in key areas around your house. For example, in my home office just over the door I have a few pictures of productivity and wealth. On my refrigerator I have some pictures of healthy foods. Over my workout room I have some motivating exercise pictures. Over my bedroom door I have some power and uplifting images. Triggers are great and work especially well after they have become a habit!

Do it With a Friend. Similar to picking a role model, if you have a friend who wants to work on the same habit, pursue it together. It's always more interesting to share your pursuits; it builds memories and gives you an opportunity to motivate each other.

Use Reminders. Sometimes your life may get so busy that all you need is a reminder to help you learn a new habit. In this day and age, setting reminders is easy. You can use post-it notes, set an alarm on your cell phone, or write it into your planner. One good technique is to align your reminders with specific places or times. For example, if you're giving up junk food, it would make sense to keep healthy food pictures on your fridge reminding you that you're trying to eat more fruits and vegetables.

Don't Give Up. One of the most important techniques is to keep on keeping on. It's the easiest thing in the world to say "forget it," and give up altogether on your pursuit. However, the more you've invested, the more it will cost you to give up. Consider all the time and effort you've invested so far, whenever you're tempted to throw in the towel. Remind yourself of why this habit is so important to you. Remember the consequences of staying the same. Visualize the end results and think about how much better your life will be once you've successfully learned the new habit. Choose afresh to claim this habit for your own, and mark your decision with an appropriate symbol as a reminder. I know I have said this before and I am going to say it later on in the book AS WELL so it sticks in. The one's who succeed are not always the best and the brightest... they are the ones who learned from their mistakes, sought out the council of those wiser than them, and those who just **NEVER GAVE UP!**

Start Small. It is easy, when you're all enthused about making change in your life, to bite off more than you can chew. It's tempting to tackle a massive global change at the beginning or to try to change everything at once. Both are recipes for disaster. It's too easy to be discouraged by the scope of the first or stressed out by the sheer quantity of details by the second. You'll be much more likely to see greater success in the long run if you start small and focus on changing one small habit at a time. For example, let's say you want to change your eating habits, you're thinking habits, and your spending habits. Instead of trying to change all three at once, pick one area and work on a single habit until it's firmly established. Then, choose another habit, either one you can build on top of the first one, or one you deem important in another area. "Step by step, the longest march can be won." (John McCutcheon)

Reward Yourself. Finally, do not be afraid to reward yourself for successfully establishing a new habit! By rewarding yourself, you give yourself something nice for all the hard work and effort you put into this accomplishment. It's a wonderful way to cap off the experience as well as acknowledging that what you've accomplished is no small feat! It can also be a powerful motivator to know you have a reward waiting for you at the end of your struggle.

Work Ethic

What is work ethic? It is an inner understanding that hard work and discipline are important. Most people who exhibit a healthy work ethic learned it from their family and those around them. If you didn't grow up around this type of example, it is easily possible to build a positive work ethic, with discipline, persistence and by developing good habits.

The people who get things done are the ones with a solid work ethic. They are the ones everyone relies on for help or good advice. They are often successful at their job and are willing to go the extra mile to finish strong! Here are some things you can do to foster a good work ethic:

Focus and Concentrate – Focus and concentration are qualities of someone with a good work ethic. These traits allow you to filter out distractions and give attention to the task at hand. This can be hard to do, but there is great focus and concentration music on YouTube for free and many other places. I personally love the Focus and Concentration download from Uncommon Knowledge! There is also a variety of focusing supplements, Ginkgo Biloba being my favorite among a variety of others.

Do it now! People with good work ethics do not wait for a better day to do things. It doesn't matter whether they feel wonderful or had a bad morning; Procrastination is not a part of their vocabulary.

People with a good work ethic will see what needs to be done and get on it right away. They have disciplined initiative. To fire up your initiative, sometimes it helps to fire up your body. This exercise may help:

Stand straight and tall, with your feet about hip distance apart, your chest high, and your eyes straight ahead. Tuck your chin slightly, while keeping your gaze straight forward. Place your hands on your hips. Take a deep breath for a count of five and feel your waist expanding. Hold for two seconds, then exhale all your breath for a count of five. Repeat the process several times.

The breathing gets your circulation going and the no-nonsense pose gives your body the idea you are ready to tackle anything. As you exhale, speak aloud one of your positive affirmations, to help focus your attitude. You can easily repeat this activity at strategic times throughout the day, whenever you need to refocus and strengthen your will to work.

Do things right. People with a solid work ethic do not just put in the minimum they can get away with. No, they complete their work thoroughly and do it right the first time so there will be no need to do things over. Nothing is done halfway or sloppily. Your work ethic will remind you to check over your work before you call it finished, even if you are in a hurry. You will accept no excuse for simple little mistakes.

Be Dependable. If you ask for something from a person with a good work ethic, chances are you will get it in a reasonable amount of time. If you tend to forget things, I suggest making up a daily "To Do" list. If you are asked for something you cannot do immediately, write it on your day's list. Your list could be in the form of physical paper or it could reside on your phone or computer. Refer to this list throughout the day, checking off items as you complete them and letting your list determine what you do next. When you don't leave things up to memory, your brainpower can be utilized for actual work and you will find you are more dependable on the job.

Be Punctual. A person with a good work ethic almost always completes a job within the deadline or shows up when expected. You will think ahead to ensure that you finish on time. A calendar app on your smart phone, ideally synced with your computer, can help you plan out your work load as well as ensuring you make it to your meetings.

Another way to set yourself up for punctuality is to prepare ahead. Lay out your clothing for the next day the night before. Pack your lunch the night before so you can grab it and go. Set out any papers or other items you will take with you. Check the weather forecast the night before to determine if you will need a coat or an umbrella, and set out those items as appropriate.

Be Productive. You can always tell the quality workers by the amount of work they complete in a workday. They usually get more done and the quality of their work is exemplary. You can increase your productivity by improving your focus, your punctuality, and all the other things we've already listed above. Before you know it, you will develop the work ethic you need to give your Big Idea a push toward reality.

People who have good work ethics have great habits and good attitudes. They are responsible and even if no one else is doing anything at work, they are the ones to get the job done. They do not depend on others, although they value and seek out help when appropriate. They accept the necessity of hard work. They apply their entire being to the job and if they come up against a barrier, they expect to be able to overcome it with innovative thinking and teamwork. They start strong by getting enough sleep the night before. They exercise and eat to fuel their bodies. They have clarity of purpose and know what their mission is in life. Finally, they take initiative and become the catalyst for their goals.

Make a good work ethic and solid personal habits your foundation. Start every task with an attitude of "I can get this done." You can see how all three of these items can benefit a big thinker. Without them, nothing you think up will ever get done.

Chapter 5: Goal-Setting and Leadership

Creating constructive goals and striving to be a good leader are two more things that are essential to thinking big and putting Big Ideas into action. How can you reach your big dream without goals? How will you pursue your goals if you are not an effective leader?

Goal-setting involves common sense and logical thinking. Your goals are the blueprints for achieving your Big Idea, so it is important to thoroughly think them through and be as specific as possible.

Setting Goals

Here are some things to consider as you set goals:

Define what you want to do. When you first start to set goals, make them big enough to encompass your Big Idea. Later, you will pare down these goals into smaller, more manageable sub-goals and objectives. Here is an example of a Big Idea with wide reach. "I will manage and own a rural bed and breakfast that will include a house for lodging and meals and a barn where special events, can take place." This objective is pretty broad, but is specific enough that you can immediately see some steps you can take to pursue it.

It is important to get to work on your Big Idea immediately. You don't want doubts to arise and derail you before you've had a chance to work out some of the practical details. I recommend you block out several hours for thinking through your Big Idea and starting to flesh out how you plan to pursue it. Find a quiet place where you can concentrate and where you will not be disturbed.

Think of what you want to accomplish from the point of view of the general public. What do you hope the reviewers will say when they critique your work? How do you expect your customers to view their experience with you? What do you hope the people who inherit your business will think of it? In other words, what do you want for your legacy?

In the case of the bed and breakfast, you might expect critics to praise the rooms as cozy, beautiful, and comfortable; you hope they rave about the extraordinary food. Their reviews would read that everyone had a wonderful time and loved staying at a working farm. They would remark on the superior quality of the food that came directly from your farm to the table. The people who stayed there would come back time and time again and become well-loved clients. You want your legacy to read that you ran the nicest bed and breakfast in three counties. The people who own your business after you will be pleased to inherit a well-maintained facility and an exquisitely managed process.

Write down your goal. Use a notebook, vision board or a computer document. Once you've gotten it written down somewhere, take a good look at your goal. Is it reasonable; that is, can the scope of your objective be accomplished in the time frame you expect? A goal of "I want to live on the moon" might not be reasonable.

State your goal in positive terms. Always say "I will" instead of "I won't". Here is a negative goal statement for that upscale restaurant idea: "I will not allow hamburgers and French fries to be served at my elegant restaurant, but will introduce fine dining to middle class families." While it states your objective, it approaches the topic from a negative perspective. Here's a more positive take: "I will serve interesting and elegant choices that might not be found on other middle-class menus, in order to expose customers to a variety of flavors and techniques for preparing food." This wording doesn't explicitly ban hamburgers, but it states in positive terms what you intend to accomplish. If you play your cards right, your customers won't even miss the burgers and fries!

Tell someone. Choose someone you trust and let him or her in on your idea and your goals. Your confidante should be someone who can be trusted to offer suggestions from a position of support. Choose someone you can bounce ideas off and who will brainstorm right along with you. You want a person who will tell you when your ideas suck, but without judging you personally, and then will dig in with you to improve them. You are much more likely to continue forward in your pursuit if you have this kind of support.

Break it down. Partition your main goal into smaller discrete steps and assign tentative deadline dates to each step or major milestone in the process. While these dates may be adjusted as situations change, they will give you something concrete to shoot for. Otherwise you may well spend the rest of your life on step one. They say that tasks expand to fill the amount of time allotted to them; deadlines can tell those tasks just how far they are allowed to expand.

Work in parallel. Some tasks naturally break down into sequences of actions that must be completed in a specific order. However, you may have large chunks of your main objective that can be developed independently from the rest of the project. In this case, you might want to break these large chunks off into separate categories and pursue their sequences simultaneously. In the case of our bed and breakfast, here are some parts of the project that could be pursued independently:

- Property and financial management

- House development and maintenance – bedrooms, kitchen, dining area

- Barn development and maintenance – kitchen, hall, dance floor

- Coordination of construction and contractors

- Landscaping and grounds maintenance

- Farming Activities

- Staffing

- Advertising and Marketing

Set an overarching goal for each category along with sub-goals. In the property category you might state one step as, "I will find a realtor and look at several properties by such-and-such a date." You really can't go any further than that step until you actually have a property to work with, but you can brainstorm and research some of the other categories, such as what kind of animals you want include in your farm. You could also rough in other categories such as a generic staffing and maintenance outline.

Set up a "TO DO" list. After each goal is defined, establish some milestone dates for the first month, six months, one year, five years and ten years.

For example, under the "Property" category, you might set up the following set of benchmark statements

- I will set up appointments with my realtor to view at least four properties in one month's time.

- By the end of six months I will have decided which property to buy.

- By the end of seven months I will have reviewed and selected the necessary financing options to purchase this property.

Review and adjust. Your goals are not written in stone. They can always be changed and your deadlines may be adjusted to fit in with reality. Goals are a motivational and planning tool. As long as you are working toward them, they will go far to help you attain your Big Idea.

Leadership

Leadership is something impossible to do justice to in just a few short paragraphs. Throughout this book we have touched on characteristics related to leadership, since leadership is ingrained in the very idea of pursuing a Big Idea. However, what follows is a direct look at leadership that should help you develop some of its basics.

Leadership is a trait every big thinker needs. How else will you move toward your goals if you can't lead yourself? If you haven't learned to lead yourself, how will you be able to lead others?

Sorry if this disappoints you, but you can't do it all yourself. You need other people if you intend to reach your dream. Leadership skills are essential if you hope to work effectively alongside others. How else will you win people to your side? How will you explain, describe, inspire, and encourage them to work with you to bring your Big Idea to reality?

You won't become an effective leader overnight, but here are some things you can do to move yourself down the road toward mature leadership:

Learn from other leaders. Look back in history to identify two to three leaders you admire. If you're drawing a blank, check into the lives of Steve Jobs, Oprah, Eleanor Roosevelt or Mother Theresa. Study the lives of your chosen leadership mentors with an eye to how they developed their leadership skills. Start a journal where you write examples of leadership that speak to you and your specific needs. Constantly look for how modern leaders are able to accomplish successes.

Be willing to experience discomfort. As a leader, you often have to do things you would rather avoid. If you run a company, you may have to let workers go on occasion; this can be very uncomfortable, even if you know it is necessary to the health of your business. You will find that turning your dream into reality will stretch you in ways you never imagined. Some of these stretching experiences will be fun, but others will be rather unpleasant and uncomfortable.

The way to deal with this discomfort is to go against your natural inclination to shrink back and instead press forward into the experience. If you are afraid to speak in front of crowds, start out small; join a toastmasters club or take a class that will include making verbal presentations. Find a Small Business Development Center near you; this US Government-sponsored service may help you as you face various hurdles and challenges to your dream. Consider any discomfort as a sign that you are growing; choose to embrace it.

Believe you are a leader and look back at your role models. Try to imagine a role model in your situation and ask yourself questions like, "What would Oprah do in this situation?" or "How would Martin Luther King, Jr. handle this problem?"

Keep learning, constantly. Key up your curiosity to learn as much about your "field of dreams" as possible. Approach every business you interact with as an opportunity to learn something. With our rural bed and breakfast example, look into popular entertainment venues and see how they became successful. Visit other B&Bs to discover how they interact with their guests. Learn everything you can about farming; visit a farm similar to your own to learn how they care for their animals and manage their crops. Become a student of your neighbors' gardens and garner tips you can use in your own. Many towns have a local garden club or an urban garden where you can volunteer your time to gain valuable skills.

Knowledge is power; that is not an empty cliché. Actively pursue what you need to know in order to build confidence in the various skills necessary to fulfill your dream. Confidence in your skills will also build your confidence in your ability to lead

Gather resources for future reference. Keep physical binders or files in your computer about what you learn. Organize them for easy access as a reference library to help you practically achieve your dream. Then, when you are able to quickly access answers to others' questions you will be laying the groundwork for them to look up to you as a leader.

Build relationships with everyone you live around and lead. No one likes a distant leader. People much more appreciate the person who takes the time to get to know them. Take your people out to lunch or meet them individually for coffee to learn about their lives and their dreams, in addition to sharing your own.

Perfect your spoken word. A leader gives clear, concise directions and explanations at the opportune time. If this is not your forte you may need to practice. Practice communicating precisely what you mean. This may entail slowing down your thoughts. For practice in slowing down your thoughts, first jot down what you want to say, then refine it. Keep to the point and move your explanation forward in a logical fashion. This exercise can be especially effective when you are facing a tricky situation or dealing with a person who calls for special care in communicating.

Visualize yourself as a leader. In your visualization speak to your coworkers and staff in order to encourage them and direct them to get the job done. This will help your goal-setting and leadership skills improve and can help you to become the person you need to be.

The video, "How To Be A Leader – Leadership Secrets Revealed" by Actualized.org, explains how leadership skills are actually a recipe for your whole life. Your leadership abilities are what helps you take care of your own needs and meet the needs of your family and the people around you. You will only see the results you want in life as you develop your leadership skills.

Chapter 6: Thirty Days to Thinking Big

In this chapter we will create a strategic plan to help you think big and put your plans into motion. First, however, we need to examine where you are and your readiness to develop this plan.

The First Exercise

Choose three things we discussed in the previous chapters of this book that you want to build into your life. You may need to overcome your fear of losing control. You may need to build your confidence or you may want to automate your life further to give you the time you need to think really big. Do you need an attitude adjustment? Are there habits you know you need to develop or replace? Is your work ethic strong? Do you need more health and vitality? Sit down by yourself or with a trusted friend and brainstorm specific things you can do to improve your three areas.

An Example

For the sake of practice, let's imagine you need these three things:

- to overcome fear of talking to people you don't know
- to increase your confidence
- to stop procrastinating

Your next task is to create steps you can take to accomplish these three objectives. You can create separate steps for each objective or you can integrate your three goals into a single event, as is described below. Here is what your plan may look like on paper. You will note that each item has a proposed time for completion. You will also note that in this example there is much overlap between the different goals and their activities.

#1 Overcome fear	#2 Increase Confidence	#3 Stop Procrastinating
By the end of this week I will tell a trusted friend what are my fears and what causes them.	*Each day* I will visualize every detail of speaking calmly and confidently before my chosen audience.	*Today* I will start calling to find a group that will let me speak to them.
By the end of next week I will have set a date and time on which to speak.	*One time each week*, I will visualize everything that could possibly go wrong when I speak to the group, from hecklers,	*This week* I will find a school or club that will let me speak to them about *(choose a topic)*.

	to forgetting what I plan to say and how I will plan to succeed in these situations.	
I will practice my speech in front of family and friends *six different times before* the scheduled date of the speech.	I will begin *each practice* speech with a few deep breaths, repeating aloud, "I am confident in my message and am perfectly comfortable around people I do not know."	I will write and practice my speech *one day after securing a date* for my performance.

Now, go build your own plan and implement it. Ideally, you should choose an action plan that will take about thirty days to complete.

Big Idea Strategy Plan

1. Write down your Big Idea. What do you want to do? Describe the vision you have for the future in a single paragraph, summarizing the characteristics you are excited to bring to fruition. Your summary should convey the specific characteristics that fired you up about this dream in the first place. This is what you are working toward. Write it down in a square at the top of your plan. Do not think small. If you start big here, your big thinking will mean something significant down the road.

2. Now that you know where you are going, you need to clearly define where you are starting from and then decide how to get from point A (where you are now) to point B (the realization of your Big Idea). Make one list detailing what you will have when you have reached your objective. Accept that this list will change as you get into the process of building your dream and better understanding the process. To simplify matters you might want to divide your list into four broad categories:

    a) Physical (property, buildings, machinery, computers, etc.)

    b) Business Management (financial planning, business structure, etc.)

    c) Skills (What somebody needs to be able to do)

    d) Knowledge (Industry standards, etc.)

3. Build another list with two columns. In one column, put down everything you already have; in the other column mark down the things you need.

4. Choose the general strategies you will need to reach your Big Idea. Create measurable steps you can check off as you go along. List your strategies in order below your summary description.

5. Each one of your strategies now needs an action plan to explain how you plan to complete it. Order your strategies sequentially and specify a timeframe for completing each one.

You might want to set things up in time increments. Start with next week, in two weeks, in one month, two months...., six months..., 1 year...., 5 years.

Once you have this framework in place, you can start implementing the plan on a daily basis. You will adjust the plan as you go along. Your strategies aren't set in concrete; they can easily be changed as you progress toward the big picture. Just remember, most great things are doing fairly quickly with massive action when the inspiration is there.

A Sample Plan

The following is an example of a Big Thinking Strategy Plan for building a chain of pet stores. Assume the person doing this has been a dog breeder and trainer for years and has the knowledge and connections to start up this store.

Big Plan:

I will open a chain of pet stores that will cater mostly to dog owners. I will open one store and after seeing how it works out, I will open another in a neighboring community. I hope to have a chain of ten stores in five years. Here potential dog owners can be put in touch with breeders; they can buy a rescue dog, purchase items needed to raise a dog, buy food, and learn how to train a dog or have it trained by staff. A vet will work in the store and will be able to perform basic surgeries. A groomer will also be located on the premises and will be available to groom dogs by appointment.

Lists

What I have to work with:

- Knowledge of breeding and training dogs
- A vet willing to work with me
- A groomer willing to work with me
- Equipment for a kennel

What I Need:

- Location and building

- Vendor for dog supplies and food
- Grooming tables
- Equipment for grooming dogs
- Equipment for vet
- Equipment for surgery for vet

Strategies

- In One Week – Develop a temporary business plan. Go to http://www.lawdepot.com/ for a business plan template.
- In One Week – Develop a list of things needed to start the business and.
- In the Second Week – Check equipment vendors and write down prices for all items I will need in order to start the business (pet tables, kennels, food bowls, water bowls, surgery tables, lamps, grooming tables, lamps, shampoo area etc).
- In the Second Week – Go to financial institutions with my plan and my lists to find out how much financing I can get.
- In Week Three – Check out possible locations with a real estate agent.
- In Week Four – Consult a lawyer to develop contracts with both vet and groomer.
- In Week Five – Establish a relationship with dog shelters and breeders.

In the following 4 to 5 months:

- Contingent upon receiving necessary financing, rent a building and procure all licenses needed for the business
- Procure all equipment needed for the store. Work on getting everything the vet and groomer need. This will be done in the next 4 months.
- Place ads for staff members in print and online job searches and hire staff. This will be done in the next 5 months.
- Set up a web page, release social media and print advertising in anticipation of opening of first store in the next 5 months.

This is just an example and your plan will most likely be more detailed. You can write down any goals you want and later put them in order. You can also detail specific categories.

The best way to follow a plan is to buy a desk calendar with big squares for days. You can also opt for a planner book. Keep your all your tasks and deadlines on this master calendar so you can see them every day.

For additional help with strategic planning, watch these informational videos: Overview of the Strategic Planning Process and What is a Strategic Plan, Really? by virtualstrategist on YouTube.

Setting up a strategic plan for your Big Idea will help you to keep on track and avoid overlooking any critical detail. Your plan gives you a blueprint for action, in order to reach the object of your big thinking.

Chapter 7: Inspirational Story- Oprah: From Poverty to a Big Life

Oprah Winfrey is considered one of the wealthiest women in America and one of the greatest philanthropists in American history. She did not get where she is today by thinking small. Oprah is a consistent big thinker who doesn't let anything diminish her drive or waylay her plans. We all can learn much from how she has lived and dreamed.

Oprah was born in Mississippi, in 1954, to a teenage single mother. She lived with her grandmother for years before moving in with her mother. Her childhood was not idyllic by any stretch of the imagination. The family lived in extreme poverty. From the age of nine, Oprah was repeatedly raped by male relatives and friends. She ran away from home when she was thirteen and at fourteen became pregnant, only to have the baby die soon after birth.

Anyone else might have given up by this time, but Oprah had an internal drive that pushed her forward. She also had a father who believed that education would make a difference in her life. When Oprah went to live with her father as a teenager, he made sure she got the education she needed. Oprah started to dream big and soon was an honor student. She was a member of the high school speech team that won a competition, which granted a full scholarship to Tennessee State University.

Oprah cemented her big dream during her senior year in high school when she started working at a local radio station. She kept this job for two years during college. Once out of college, she landed a news anchor position in Nashville and then in Baltimore. The critics flocked to her side. Oprah was frequently criticized for her appearance. Critics also said she lacked the journalistic expertise held by white males in the field. One went so far as to say she was unfit for television. Another fired her.

That did not stop Oprah. She had her sights set on becoming a household name. She took a job at a morning talk show in Chicago and eventually was put in a slot opposite the Phil Donahue show. No one thought she would be noticed in light of the big-name competition, but people liked Oprah's style and grace. In a short period of time she had outshone Donahue's ratings.

Oprah has obviously reached her initial goal. She became a household name, but she didn't stop there. She started dreaming greater dreams and making bigger plans. She syndicated her own show, running it from 1986 to 2011. She launched O Magazine with the Hearst Corporation and since then her big thinking has led her to begin her own TV network. All this, from a woman who had been deemed "unfit for television."

But that's not all. Oprah started to think big about helping other people. Oprah's Angel Network began in 1988 and raised over $3.5 million by asking viewers for donations. The Network gave away over 150 $25,000 scholarships and counting. Oprah didn't just ask viewers for their money; she asked for their time. Volunteers responded by the score, building many homes with Habitat for Humanity.

The Angel Network ceased operation in 2010, but in its lifetime it raised over 80 million dollars and helped victims of hurricanes Rita and Katrina, building 60 schools in 13 different countries and insuring that their students had the books and uniforms they needed.

Oprah has donated about 400 million dollars to education and $40 million to her Leadership Academy for girls in South Africa. She is thinking big once again and beefing up her charitable organizations so her big thinking and big ideas can benefit even more people in the future. I love the "OWN" in her company name. In today's modern age, it is very powerful to own the full rights to your creations!

This little girl born into poverty with a violent early childhood was honored by President Barack Obama with the presidential Medal of Freedom in 2013. That is what thinking big and never giving up can do!

Chapter 8: Ace's Ultimate Bonus Tips

The best time to Think Big is when you are at your best; however you never know when inspiration may strike. But chances are, inspiration will strike most often when you are healthy, doing the right things and working hard towards your goals. In this section I'll give you some of my personal success secrets that will help you perform to the best of your abilities and get into the "Flow" state of mind. Be sure to use the strategies that fit into your life the best and take the time to devise your own personal success strategy based off of your personal strengths and how you would like things in your life to go.

1. Have a morning routine. An incredible strategy that many of today's new hot peak performers are using is a morning routine. This includes a variety of things that you will do every morning in order to get yourself and your body ready for the day in the best way possible. Be sure to design your own morning ritual that will get you ready for the day. For example some of the things that I will do every day include waking up, doing some deep breathing, and then putting on a smile as I start the day. I will then open the blinds in my house while thinking of all the things that I'm grateful for. The next thing I will do is drink either a large glass of water or large glass of water filled with a super green food formula powder. I will then bounce up and down on a mini trampoline while using deep breathing techniques up to 20 deep breaths alternating between my nose and my mouth. I then like to take a few minutes to go through my goals and then watch some quick positive videos. I have a whole library of videos from YouTube and other sources that are either motivational or success driven that are great to watch in the morning. I would advise taking the time to research whatever you are interested in and then making your own personal library of great videos that you can watch. I find around 3 to 6 minute videos are the best. One of my favorites is the Millionaire Mindset Subliminal by jamz subliminals on YouTube. I will then eat a light breakfast usually consisting of a banana and spinach blended into a quick smoothie or a muscle milk protein shake. I will take my vitamins and minerals and other supplements after this. I then go out on a short walk around my neighborhood and then come back and do about 10-20 minutes of quick work on the most important task of the day determined by my geniusly designed 80/20 plan of action. I then like to go into my backyard and stretch out my whole body while visualizing my current goals being accomplished. That is basically my morning ritual; it may change from day to day, but not by too much. Be sure to design your own if you want to really be performing in your life the way you want to be. On a scale of 1-10 of things you need to do in order to really get things done in your life... I would say this is about a level 10.

2. If you are really hardcore and want to succeed no matter what, then a good strategy is to either jump in some very cold water or to take a cold shower. This will shock your body and you will find that you will be more awake and performing much better after this. For example, right before editing this book, I jumped into my freezing cold pool and then took a cold shower right after that. This immediately woke my whole body up and got me ready to perform at my best.

3. In order to think big, you will find it much easier if you are eating properly and exercising properly. I know you've heard this a million times, but it is much easier to perform at your best and get into flow states of mind when your body and mind are performing like well-oiled machines. I won't be going into huge details on this, but if this is something that you want help with then my book Ultimate Health Secrets will give you everything you need as far as your health goes.

4. Be sure to eliminate negative influences from your life. You want to surround yourself with positive and uplifting people who are going to support your dreams and goals. You got better things to do than worry about the limiting beliefs of others. It is much easier to succeed when you are in a positive environment full of success minded people. You can see this in almost every aspect of professional sports and business. It is truly incredible what a good team of people can accomplish together!

5. Mastermind groups are an extremely powerful way to help you succeed in your goals and dreams. These types of groups have been around for thousands of years and isn't something new. But those who have been able to form powerful alliances or mastermind groups and work together for a common goal have been able to do absolutely amazing things throughout the history of human civilization for the past several thousand years. I would highly recommend either joining a mastermind group or doing what I did, and just form your own. There are a lot of different strategies that people use for mastermind groups, but the best I have ever seen is summed up quite beautifully by Pat Flynn in his YouTube video "How To Build A Winning Mastermind Group."

6. Make a list that is filled with all of your great accomplishments throughout your life. Sometimes it is easy to forget all of the incredible things we have done over time. Be sure to make a list of all the great experiences and things you have done and then be sure to go over them at least once a week to remind yourself of all the great things you have done and what you can do.

7. Develop a power routine that will help get you in a Thinking Big frame of mind. A power routine can be almost anything that you can imagine, but it should be something that you could do fairly quickly in order to

get you into a better frame of mind so that you can perform at peak performance. One thing many people do will be a physical ritual that gets them locked in and ready to perform. Baseball players are famous for this; you'll see a lot of them doing the same ritual over and over again before each swing of the bat. NLP techniques are great for helping program certain body movements to getting ready to perform at whatever task needs to be done. One of my personal favorite rituals that I designed myself can be done very easily. Whenever I am ready to start working, I'll snap my fingers two times real quick and then give a thumbs up and then snap my fingers real quick two times again and then give another thumbs-up. After that it's go time. Your power routine can be anything, from turning around in a circle then pumping your hand down into a fist, or pounding yourself on the chest, or just a couple taps of the foot mixed with a powerful phrase in your head, or whatever makes you happy and works for you. Your power routine should get you immediately motivated and ready to take action.

8. A powerful team is usually the result of someone who has been able to think big. The greatest people in history have had the ability to build a powerful team! Just look at all the kings who had powerful noble allies. With all the incredible improvements in technology, it is much easier to build a team than ever before! Your team can include friends, family members, employees, internet friends, and even the general public. In order to truly do great things in your life, you're going to need to outsource the majority of tasks that you are not great in. My favorite place to do this for business needs is www.Upwork.com. Here you can get a variety of virtual assistants who can help you. Just take a look at all of the powerful corporations around the world and see how they use the power of other people to help make them into global juggernauts. Trying to do everything yourself nowadays is a losing proposition. You're better off building a powerful team of smart and trusted allies who can do their jobs well to help you and your team win. I would not be as successful as I am today without a great team behind me! For expert analysis on how to build a winning team then be sure to check out my powerful book on Team Building.

9. Hard Work is what it will always take to be truly successful. Not only will it take hard work, but you have to realize that in many cases, it is going to be between 4 and 12 times harder than you think it will be to succeed in your goals! You can be the greatest person in the world at thinking big, but if there is no action behind your thoughts than nothing is going to get done. In the future, things will get easier as your hard work pays off, but realize that you're just always going to have to work hard and do things right to continue producing success after success and victory after victory. Those who have been unbelievably successful on this planet tend to have a strong desire to succeed with a powerful willpower to just not give up until victory is attained. You really have never lost out on a goal until you have given

up on it. Arnold Schwarzenegger, one of my great role models, sums up the principle of working hard very nicely in my favorite YouTube video of all time: "[The Six Secrets To Success (New)](#)" by Travis Fisher. To truly be successful, you have to put in the work. This hard work will help you immensely as you grow older. I will say that the greatest investment of my life has been in health and fitness. I have spent thousands upon thousands of dollars on my health, and worth every penny! Father time can be a ruthless adversary, so fight the good fight when you can and whenever you can! Never give up, believe in yourself and **THING BIG**! You only live once... how do you want to be remembered in the pages of history?

Conclusion

I hope this book was able to help you see all the benefits there are to Thinking Big!

The next step is to take the time to start thinking big every day so you can develop a Big Idea that can help you realize your dreams. You may be the next Donald Trump, the next Oprah Winfrey, or the next J.K. Rowling. You could be one of the most successful artists or writers of the 21st century. You could be the richest individual in the world. You could have a chain of restaurants, bakeries, hotels, bed and breakfasts, or resorts. You could be living on a private island in a giant castle bringing in a giant passive income with all the luxuries of the modern world at your beck and call. Now is the time to start working on your 30 day plan and pursuing your Big Idea with dogged determination.

Believe in yourself. When you do, things start to fall into place. Build your confidence and overcome your fears. Let your bold, fearless self think even bigger thoughts. Automate your life so that you have more time and space to think big and pursue Big Ideas. Build up a positive attitude and lay a foundation of good habits to support your future success. Prepare to use challenges, difficulties, and the occasional setback to your advantage, turning them into opportunities to grow and shine. Cultivate a strong work ethic well before you begin to implement your specific strategies. Strategize your little heart out then make a plan of action that puts the most important things to accomplish at the top of your success accomplishments list. It might take some hard work, but you can do this. Develop the qualities of a leader so that you are prepared to walk through the doors that your Big Idea has opened. Life is too short to be giving up on your dreams! If you have a burning dream in your heart then go get it! Don't give up. Separate from those who don't believe in you and form your own dream team that is hungry and ready to challenge this world! Dig deep down and just make a choice to never give up until you have won, no matter how long it takes! If you keep doing the right things then you will Succeed!

Finally, if you discovered at least one thing that has helped you or that you think would be beneficial to someone else, be sure to take a few seconds to easily post a quick positive review. As an author, your positive feedback is desperately needed. Your highly valuable five star reviews are like a river of golden joy flowing through a sunny forest of mighty trees and beautiful flowers! *To do your good deed in making the world a better place by helping others with your valuable insight, just leave a nice review.*

My Other Books and Audio Books
www.AcesEbooks.com

Peak Performance Books

Health Books

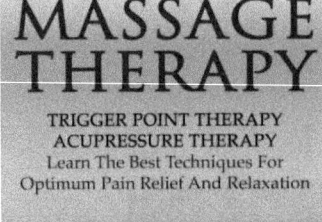

Be sure to check out my audio books as well!

 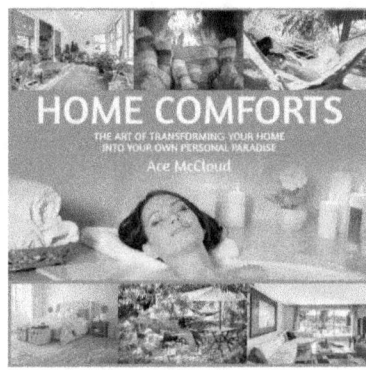 

Check out my website at: **www.AcesEbooks.com** for a complete list of all of my books and high quality audio books. I enjoy bringing you the best knowledge in the world and wish you the best in using this information to make your journey through life better and more enjoyable! **Best of luck to you!**

www.ingramcontent.com/pod-product-compliance
Lightning Source LLC
Chambersburg PA
CBHW051425070526
44584CB00023B/3589